Life Lessons *from* Biblical Encounters

A Great Insight to a Spiritual Turning Point

Abigael Akintola

ISBN 978-1-64416-406-8 (paperback)
ISBN 978-1-64416-407-5 (digital)

Copyright © 2018 by Abigael Akintola

All rights reserved. No part of this publication may be reproduced, distributed, or transmitted in any form or by any means, including photocopying, recording, or other electronic or mechanical methods without the prior written permission of the publisher. For permission requests, solicit the publisher via the address below.

Christian Faith Publishing, Inc.
832 Park Avenue
Meadville, PA 16335
www.christianfaithpublishing.com

Printed in the United States of America

To the glory of God and the Triune as the first fruit of His calling in my life.

Contents

Foreword..7

Acknowledgements..9

Introduction..11

Chapter 1. Jabbok...15

Chapter 2. God's Expectation 21

Chapter 3. A Call to Service..................................25

Chapter 4. Strategic Placement 28

Chapter 5. The Great Catch 31

Chapter 6. At Master's Feet...................................35

Chapter 7. Inside Out...38

Chapter 8. Bad Credit History..............................42

Chapter 9. An Altered Vessel.................................46

Conclusion..51

FOREWORD

When Abigael approached me to write the foreword for her book, I welcomed the opportunity with excitement and anticipation.

I have known Abigael for several years. I have had the opportunity to minister with her in several programs and events. I have known her as a passionate woman with a heart for God and His kingdom. I have come to know her as a woman of God who is called as a voice to the next generation. So when she told me about the book, I was excited for her because I believe that through the book, she has the unique opportunity to communicate a message God has put in her heart to bless the world.

On the other hand, I was full of anticipation because of the title of the book. When she told me that the focus of the book is on lessons from biblical encounters of different individuals in the Bible, I was eagerly looking forward to learning from what the Holy Spirit was going to unveil through her on a subject that I believe is pivotal to our journey of faith. And having gone through the manuscript, I wasn't disappointed at the unique insight and revelation that God has given her about some biblical characters and their encounters with the Lord.

Beginning with her own personal encounter with God, she later invited the reader to an expository journey on the encounters of diverse individuals in the Bible such as Jacob, Hannah, Samuel, Elijah and Elisha, Apostle Peter, Mary (the sister of Martha), Zacchaeus, the thief at the cross, and Saul of Tarsus (who later became Paul). She masterfully unveils the impact of an encounter with God on their individual lives and points out the key lessons for us today.

The author leaves the reader with no doubt that an encounter with God produces freedom from guilt, shame, and weaknesses of their past; a miraculous experience and testimony; a sense of God's call and purpose; a call to sacrifice and discipleship; spending time in the presence of God; life transformation; and ultimately salvation and drawing nearer to God.

While our individual experiences and encounter with God may be unique and personal, I equally believe that none of the challenges we face in life in our walk with God are unique to us. Hence, there are vital lessons and nuggets we can glean about God from the experiences of others who have gone ahead of us. That is why the Bible in Romans 15:4 says, "For whatsoever things were written aforetime were written for our learning, that we through patience and comfort of the scriptures might have hope."

I believe this book would expose you to vital lessons about having an encounter with God but, at the same time, challenge you to set the right atmosphere for a unique encounter with God. One encounter with God can change the course of the rest of your life and set you on the path of fulfillment of your purpose on earth.

Shalom!
Dr. Johnson Iyilade
Founder, Faith Life Community

ACKNOWLEDGEMENTS

I am much indebted to my husband, Ezekiel Akintola, for his moral support, encouragement, and for believing in the gifts of God in my life.

My appreciation goes to my parents, Overseer and Deaconess Samson O. Oludeyi, for their support and encouragement at all times. They realized this gift when it was birthed, and they encouraged me to improve on it. I love you, Dad and Mom.

My gratitude also goes to my siblings—Rebecca Adewole, Cornelius, Juliana, and Gideon Oludeyi—for their love and for being my best friends from childhood.

And to my little princess, I love you so much. You are indeed an extension of God's love to me.

I cannot but appreciate everyone who has participated in my success story.

Words cannot express my gratitude to Dr. Johnson Iyilade for his advice and support to fore-word this manuscript.

INTRODUCTION

At every stage in life, we come across different people or events that leave footprints in our hearts, either positively or negatively, of the ways through which God draws us closer is encounter. However, every Christian filled with the Holy Spirit have had a spiritual encounter with God at one time or another. Most people may not recognize it as such because it's not spectacular like that of some biblical characters. For example, at conversion, when the old man was crucified with Christ, and a new man was born, that was a spiritual encounter. The full impact of that encounter, however, become evident as you grow in your walk with God, relationship with others, and in your work for God.

Furthermore, when we study the word of God, and we receive a revelation or insight into our spirit man, the Word transforms us and changes our perspective on God and His ways. That's also a spiritual encounter!

Divine encounters often happen when we least expected. An encounter is not magical but supernatural. It can never be created by men, but you can create an avenue to be a recipient of it. There were a couple of times that I woke up feeling a paradigm shift in my life without talking to anyone. I remember waking up with a repentant heart after I had an encounter a few years ago. I knew I'd encountered God in my dream. I came to realize how distant I had been from God due to the daily busyness of activities. I had strayed so far away in my relationship with God. I attended church services every Sunday, but there was more that needed to be done. I knew it, but there were tons of things to do, I guess I had a misplaced priority. The Spirit of God convinced me to draw nearer to God. I was so sorrowful for distancing myself from God, who is my first priority.

My elder sister came to my room and found me crying, my pillow was soaked with tears. She asked if I received a call from anyone that brought tears to my eyes because we were living together in the house, so no one would have come into the house without her knowledge. I told her I was remorseful for my actions by being too busy for God instead of being busy with Him. Before that day, I hardly heard God speak to me the way He does because I had lost touch with the signal. I will relate this to a radio network whereby there is a reception failure not because there is no signal, but because the receiver is not strategically located where it can receive the signal. In the same manner, God is always sending the signal through speaking, but when we are too busy for God, we don't receive the signal. He is always speaking to us as He speaks to other Christians, but when our antenna is wrongly located or not tuned in, it will always be lost.

Other people will continue to make the best use of their radios while ours will not work. God is always speaking to His children, but what happens when we lose signal or are placed in a non-receptive environment? The world will receive the signal, but we will be left out, so the solution is to connect and relocate to the source and in this case, God. My sister admonished me to always make God my priority in the midst of my busy schedule. I was filled with great joy, and an overwhelming peace flooded my heart that day onward. My second experience was similar, but this time, with a mandate for the kingdom work.

> But seek first the kingdom of God and His righteousness, and all these things shall be added to you. (Matthew 6:33)

The Spirit of God ministered to me to put everything else aside and to always seek the kingdom of God while He attends to all my secondary needs. I have seen God come true for me on this. When we seek and run after the kingdom business, all other things start to fall into place. We need not run after material things because they will become an addition to us. I have had series of encounters, and they are always impactful.

How then do you know you have had an encounter with the one you do not know? This brings us to the essence of this book where I will be sharing life lessons from biblical encounters with much focus on the events, recipients, and outcomes of these experiences. We will be challenged on things we need to know and do to be a continuous recipient of spiritual encounter.

Chapter 1

Jabbok

Jacob, whose promised new name, Israel, remained with his descendants, and the land he was promised by God until this present day was a patriarch. It was a long road to Jacob's encounter with God. Jacob started his wrestling match from the womb of his mother where he wrestled with his brother, Esau, an act to be the firstborn of the family. He was named Jacob, which is translated as supplanter, schemer, and cheater. In the ancient history of Hebrew, every name is tagged with the child's identity. In his effort to be received the blessing of the firstborn, he contended with Esau to get his birthright and conspired with his mother to obtain the blessings from his father through deceit. Jacob also went further to wrestle with his uncle Laban to obtain flocks, herds, and his daughters, although Laban made him pay dearly for everything. And finally, Jacob wrestled with a divine being, God. What a life!

The events that led to Jacob's encounter with God was unpleasant because it was a result of him deceitfully taking his brother's birthright, and Esau's response was to kill Jacob once he is found. Hearing this, Jacob did what every other person would do, by fleeing for his life. On his way to his uncle's house in Haran, when the sun had set, he found a place to rest, and God's presence was with him there. This was where God introduced Himself to Jacob as the God of his grandfather Abraham and father, Isaac. Although God did not condone Jacob's illicit act, He had chosen him before he was born. God gave him promises about his descendants and assurance to be with him.

At Bethel, Jacob was all alone resting on a stone while asleep, he had left his comfort zone. But in his dream, he saw a ladder connecting heaven to earth with angels ascending and descending, then he saw God visiting him. This ladder is a connection that only God provides to link Himself to man. It is impossible for a man to create an encounter with God; we can only be expectant to be visited by God as opposed by the men of Babel who wanted to build a tower to heaven. When he woke up from his dream, he realized God was with him, and he named the place "Bethel," making a promise of tenth of his possessions to God upon a successful sojourn.

> Then Jacob made a vow, saying, "If God will be with me, and keep me in this way that I am going, and give me bread to eat and clothing to put on, so that I come back to my father's house in peace, then the Lord shall be my God. And this stone which I have set as a pillar shall be God's house, and of all that You give me I will surely give a tenth to you." (Genesis 28:20–22)

He made a vow with four requests; God's presence, protection, food, and clothing, but God gave him spiritual inheritance with the blessings of family, animals, and male and maidservants. Jacob, unlike his brother, was not an outdoor person and a tough adventurer, but he served his uncle Laban for years until it was set time to return home to meet with his brother whom he had cheated. All through Jacob's journey of twenty years in exile, his identity was unknown to him. Isaac was dead, he was never to see his mother again, and his only brother is his worst enemy. He called on the God of Abraham and Isaac because he was yet to identify his God. Jacob sent his family, animals, and servants across the river ahead to Esau while he promised to join them.

> Then Jacob was left alone; and a Man wrestled with him until the breaking of day. (Genesis 32:24)

At night, he was all alone. Jacob was stripped of everything he had, all what he had worked for all through his twenty years in exile, his sacrifices, pain, services, and identity. What then becomes of Jacob's identity when all is gone and none is left? He was in solitude. He was filled with the consequences of his past and the reality of the present and future. The fear of rejection and destruction from Esau was mounting up within him. His conscience and memories came alive left with memories of the past and the uncertainty of the future. His bag of scams is exhausted, no strategies, no deceit, and no scheme. He was in a state of privacy. No more disguise; the voice becomes the voice of Jacob, no animal skin for disguise, the odor is the scent of Jacob, clothes become Jacob's clothes, and at this point, Jacob is under God's spotlight. No hiding place and no secret with no other choice than to identify his true identity.

We all need to come to this state in our lives where God's spotlight is on us, no disguise, and no hideout, stripped of every disguise, thereby acknowledging our weaknesses to fully identify with Christ. We humans are not likely to be deprived of power and personal strength without struggles, but until we realize that our scheme, human reasoning, and thoughts are limited to God's plans for us, we keep struggling and wrestling with life. Oftentimes, I find myself in solitude when every wall—phones, people, activities, events, and everything else—are not available mostly in the night, and the only person to talk to is God, this is the time I am faced up to my own individuality, exploring, soul searching, mood, and reflection. There is a need to always ask yourself about your identity: who am I? Who is my soul? Who am I without my spouse, children, family, career, ministry, and everything else?

God wanted Jacob to have a soul-searching experience in his life journey, a state of knowing who you are, and what you represent when you are stripped from everything that you personally think gives you identity. There are quite a lot of lessons from Jacob's encounter with the divine being, God. Jacob encountered God in his low estate when he was down to nothing and all alone. God is a merciful God who does not want to keep us waiting, so God appeared small in size, in a form of a man familiarizing Himself with the frailty of men. God gave him the opportunity to search and find himself that he could lose everything he had labored for. Jacob knew he had no one to turn to except God. The lives of his children, wives, animals, and servants are at stake if Esau decides to kill them.

Jacob wouldn't have wrestled with God at Bethel on his way to Haran because he was a weak man, not fortified and strengthened by God. Over the years, Jacob had developed external strength, as his internal strength was developing. God had empowered and strengthened Jacob that he was able to wrestle with the divine being. This is an illustration that when we work with God in faith and obedience, He builds us up internally and externally to do the impossible. God dealt with him by inserting a painful thorn in his flesh, he had never met a man stronger than himself, and now he is challenged in the area of his might to a trial of strength with a divine being.

God wanted Jacob to know that he ought not to be afraid of his encounter with Esau, rather with God, his God. He wanted Jacob to realize that strength comes from God and the means to go with the fight. God wrestled with him to conquer his unregenerate spirit, subdue his flesh, bless him, and make him know and acknowledge his weaknesses as a mere man whose strength is in God. God was working in Jacob to redirect his steps, change his perspectives, and to empty him. Jacob knew God to be God of Abraham and Isaac, but God wanted to be known as God of Jacob, so He needed all of Jacob which He got through the wrestling.

Everyone had struggled or wrestled with life, we lean on the weak strength of men, trying to do things in our own way, and the result has always been the same. Self-dependence is only rooted and limited in our human strength. We cannot give more than our capacity as humans, but until we get to the banks of Jabbok, we will always experience the same level of limitation, fear, and failure. There are lot of issues in life to deal with; financial, family, relationships, career, ministry, fear, and no sense of purpose, which drives us to the path of the one whose capacity is unlimited, God. We should come to a place of rest whereby we stop wrestling and trusting in God.

You may be like Jacob today: you are all alone, lonely, fearful, and scared of the future, not knowing what lies ahead. You should ask yourself this question—do I want to continue wrestling? Until you come to the end of yourself and accept the lordship of Jesus, acknowledging him as your God, you will keep struggling with life issues. Like Jacob, you need to come to a place of rest in God, trusting Him for safety. Jacob was called by a new name which God designated; he was no longer Jacob the Supplanter but Israel, a nation. Have you been tagged unworthy names, or your identity has been messed up? When you come to the arms of the God of Israel, He will give you a new identity, like He did for Jacob.

> And the Gentiles shall see thy righteousness, and all kings thy glory: and thou shalt be called by a new name, which the mouth of the LORD shall name. (Isaiah 62:2)

Jabbok is a place of diffusing, pouring out, and it means "to empty itself." This was where Jacob renounced his scheming idol and won his lifetime victory. Jabbok is a lonely place where you are faced with your inner being and God. No preacher, no counselor, no friend, and no family, just you and God. You will cross Jabbok alone—it's a personal war between you and your God, surrendering every idol that seems to exalt itself above God to the greater one, God. It was at this location that God made himself known to Jacob as his God and not just the God of Abraham and Isaac.

Are you ready to empty yourself to put on the strength and fullness of God for greater adventure in life? God's expectation of us is to be known as our God and not just the God of our fathers, either biological or fathers in faith. Not disputing that the God of our fathers is worthy to be served, but when you have a personal encounter with God, He becomes your God. Your confidence is built, your trust is unshakeable, and your relationship with him becomes intimate. This is what God desires. Are you willing to yield to the call of your father for fellowship, communion, and intimate relationship?

Response

Esau whom Jacob dreaded so much ran toward him to embrace him. Jacob's fear and worst enemy welcomed him with joy. Jacob experienced peace and safety, every of his fears were gone, and he became the patriarch of his descendants. Today we call the God of Abraham, Isaac, and Jacob. These were the three generations of Patriarchs of faith.

Challenge

Where and when is your solitude? Oftentimes, when God desires to empty us of ourselves, we are busy with a lot of things; and because many people have built walls between themselves and God, they remain in the Haran phase of their lives instead of being emptied at Jabbok to cross over to a place of rest where all life struggles have been dealt with by God.

Chapter 2

God's Expectation

When God's expectations meet our desire, or when our desires soothe God's purpose for our lives, the outcome is fulfillment. It is possible to desire a gift from God for personal pleasure outside God's purpose. God gives us what He deems necessary that we don't, but we rather believe in what we want. Some things are important but not necessary, they are called luxury. Most times, we desire luxuries for show-off, which God believes is not the best for us. As a timeless and ageless God, He blesses us at his own perfect timing. He is never late but rather on time because He doesn't use our timelines as humans. Therefore, we ought to focus on birthing God's expectations and not our expectations. Oftentimes, we feel there are vacuums in our lives that need to be filled with an idolized desire. However, God expects us to seek him in the process to know what he desires for us.

Misplaced Expectation

We all have misplaced expectations of how things will turn out. Like the case of Hannah, she desired a son who would liberate her from barrenness and reproach. God's desires for Hannah was not to bring forth an ordinary son but a prophet that would liberate God's nation from darkness and corrupt religion. God's purpose always exceeds human reasoning and capacity because He is not limited to our wildest or greatest imagination. We place a cap on our lives when we limit God's power to our thoughts. God's plans are, in infinite ways, greater than our thoughts. We need not box God up with our mediocre thoughts. If Hannah had known the fruitfulness package God had planned for her, the reproach from Peninnah would be the least of her problem.

> For as the heavens are higher than the earth, so are my ways higher than your ways, and my thoughts than your thoughts. (Isaiah 55:9)

New Approach

What is wrong with doing things the old-fashioned way? We often get accustomed to our traditional way of doing things even if it is not working out. Yearly, Elkanah, Hannah's husband, traveled to Shiloh with his family to worship and offer sacrifices to God. This was their family's traditional way of doing things over the years. Elkanah showed his love to Hannah through generosity by giving her special sacrifice during their visits to Shiloh even though she was without a child. Peninnah, Hannah's rival who always rubbed it on her, reminded her of her barrenness, and this always haunted Hannah. God uses our problems or opposition to push us out of our comfort zone to a realm of the extraordinary. Hannah didn't compete with Peninnah; she didn't have any weapon of competition anyway. Rather she was trusting God for her own blessing without bitterness toward Peninnah. Hannah had been making sacrifices and praying to God about her barrenness every year, but that year, her rival provoked her to the level of seeking God. A level that transformed her life and provided a prophet to Israel.

Likewise, the case of Hagar who provoked Sarah until Sarah made Abraham send Hagar and Ishmael away. Abraham would have been contented with Ishmael as the covenant child. Problems, oppositions, and enemies challenge us to pray and grow into the level God desires us to be.

Surprisingly, when we have a long-term problem or illness, and we have prayed about it, and it still persists, we decide in our hearts to pray about it in a shallow manner. And most times, we get comfortable with them by accepting those problems as the will of God. Elkanah summed it up that he is worth more than ten sons to Hannah even though she's barren. He thought Hannah ought to be comforted that he is always there for her. Elkanah already developed feelings for her barrenness, and he settled for it, but Hannah's hunger and thirst for a biological child were immeasurably deep.

Winston Churchill in his words states that "if you are going through hell, keep going and never, never, never give up."

Hannah did not give up but intensified more effort into seeking the God of Israel like never before. What length are you willing to go in seeking God beyond the ordinary but to a level of a great encounter?

Old familiar way always feels effortless, so why not try a new approach? It is when we hit rock bottom that we settle for the needful that produces better results.

Deep Calls to Deep

A devoted heart is a place where deep calls unto deep. Seeking God starts with a willing heart that thirsts for fellowship with the Holy Spirit. Intercession may be corporate work, but seeking God is a personal walk. It was in this state that Hannah was when she prayed in her heart with her lips moving but an unheard voice. Most times in seeking God, we encounter opposition, discouragements, problems, but our zeal to know God should grow beyond this resistance. These problems are distractions which hinder us from focusing on God's plans. As a result of Hannah's encounter in Shiloh, she prophesied who Samuel would be; a Nazarene, serving God all his life. When we catch the revelation of what God wants to do, we begin to prophesy them into existence. At that point, we would have moved from making a covenant to a realm of the spirit where we are praying the very heart of God to come true. God downloaded the blueprint of His will to our heart, and we grow from a place of prayer to having a revelation knowledge of God's expectations.

Response

There is always a miracle, an experience, and testimony which comes with every encounter with Christ. It may seem as if Samuel would have no place in the temple of God because the Levites were the known priests that minister to God. Samuel was from Ephraim's lineage, but God's plan emerged to change human laws. Samuel also had his personal encounter with God in his life's journey. He was the prophet who anointed the first two kings in Israel.

Challenge

Let your heart be conformed to the perfect will of God through the renewing of your heart and transformation of your mind in a place of prayer and meditation.

> And be not conformed to this world: but be ye transformed by the renewing of your mind, that ye may prove what is that good, and acceptable, and perfect, will of God. (Romans 12:2)

CHAPTER 3

A Call to Service

When God downloaded the blueprint of His will in Hannah's heart, she prophesied who Samuel would be, a Nazarene. Samuel was a product of Hannah's encounter at Shiloh. His life was committed to the service of the temple and the Prophet, Eli. In those days, the voice of the Lord was rare, so Samuel never had the opportunity to hear God speak. God's words came as a warning or judgement in those times. While Samuel was lying down, he heard a voice calling him, but he thought it was Eli. He approached Eli twice, but Eli told him he didn't call him. And the third time, Eli understood it was the Lord calling Samuel, so he told him to respond with, "Speak, Lord, for your servant is listening." God's words to Samuel was about a punishment to the household of Eli. This encounter with God brought about his personal experience of God as a holy and righteous God who hates sinful acts.

Being born to a praying woman, living in the house of God, and being mentored by the prophet of God was not a qualification to have a relationship with God until God called Samuel to have a personal relationship with him. You may be born into a Christian home, raised by godly parents, be a regular churchgoer, but you need to have a closer relationship with God to set the course of your life in motion. This is always a turning point.

> Now Samuel did not yet know [or personally experience] the Lord, and the word of the

Lord was not yet revealed [directly] to him. (1 Samuel 3:7, AMP)

Eli's sons would have succeeded him but because of their unrighteous act which God despised, God raised the young Samuel to succeed Eli. Although Samuel was already serving in the temple, God's call to Samuel was to deliver His message to Eli that God has decided to punish him and his sons, who will never be God's priests. Samuel continued his service under the supervision of Eli until God's affirmation of him as a prophet.

> Now Samuel grew; and the Lord was with him and He let none of his words fail [to be fulfilled]. And all Israel from Dan [in the north] to Beersheba [in the south] knew that Samuel was appointed as a prophet of the Lord. And the Lord continued to appear in Shiloh, for the Lord revealed Himself to Samuel in Shiloh by the word of the Lord. (1 Samuel 3:19–21, AMP)

After Eli's death, Samuel became the leader of God's people to fulfill the mandate of God by announcing God's word to the nation of Israel.

Response

Although Samuel was ministering to the Lord without knowing Him, God revealed Himself to Samuel and ordained him as a prophet to the nation of Israel. Samuel became the chief judge of Israel winning victories over Israel's enemies and called the nation to repentance.

Challenge

What is God's call on your life? What is your response to God's call to service? Obedience to the call of God is a great gain. God is seeking for hearts ready and willing to do His work effectively and truthfully.

Chapter 4

Strategic Placement

There has always been a transition from one state to another. However, the period of transition is always powerful. There are transitions from one government to the next all over the world today, and some recorded violence while some experienced peace depending on the parties involved. I remember the last transition of power from one government officials to another in the United States, it was the head news in the media houses and social media. The news of the election started trending before and continued afterwards, even beyond the geographical borders of the country.

A transition can be gradual or sudden, and it lasts for a differing period of time depending on the acceptance and willingness of people to adapt to the new position. For some people, coping with change is shaped by either nature or nurture events. Miriam Kaufman stated that "people spend their childhood learning to be like their parents and their adolescence learning who they are and how they are different from their parents." Permit me to say that transition from childhood to adolescence is far beyond the transformation we see with our bare eyes.

In this chapter, the focus is passing the mantle of power to the next generation, and the process involved. One would have expected the call of Elisha to be dramatic as a prophet. However, it was that of a servanthood to being a successor. Elisha, plowing twelve yokes of oxen by driving the twelfth pair himself, indeed had a bigger capacity in terms of strength. Elijah saw something spectacular in him, likewise the gifting of God in our lives. While Elijah put his cloak on Elisha, Elisha understood the symbol of Elijah's action as a call to service which he embraced. One would know that Elisha was wealthy being the owner of twelve yokes of oxen, but he left all the riches to follow Elijah who had little or nothing to give him materially.

Leaving his comfort zone to an unknown destination was a big sacrifice Elisha was willing to make to be a servant of the prophet of his Lord. Elisha left the farm plow to receive the spiritual plow of the kingdom business. He was a persistent man in fulfilling his mandate with the plow on the farm, never to lose focus or be discouraged, one attribute that helped him while his master was being taken away. He had every opportunity to stay back, but he persisted until he got a double portion of his master's anointing.

Elijah was taken up to heaven in a whirlwind but before the event, there was a transition of power from Elijah to Elisha. In preparation for Elijah's departure, being the master, Elijah told Elisha to stay behind while he fulfills the divine assignment in Bethel, but Elisha had a strong determination to follow Elijah, and this decision changed Elisha's ministry.

> Then Elijah said to Elisha, "Stay here; the LORD has sent me to Bethel. As surely as the LORD lives and as you live, I will not leave you." So they went down to Bethel. (2 Kings 2:2)

Although the prophets at Bethel and Jericho told Elisha about his master being taken away from him, Elisha remains focused and determined. Distractions may come up from anyone, but a decisive heart focuses on the goal. While the sons of prophet look on, Elijah struck the Jordan River with his cloak, and the water parted ways, and they both work on the dry ground. Elijah made Elisha an offer of what he wanted before he is being taken from him.

Surprisingly, Elisha asked for a double portion of Elijah's spirit, and he did receive it. As an affirmation to this transition, Elisha parted Jordan River with Elijah's cloak which had fallen from him, and the prophets who were watching testified that the spirit of Elijah is resting on Elisha. It was not an easy transition but through persistent spirit, Elisha got what he requested. Elisha was recognized as Elijah's replacement, thereby possessing the authority and certification of Elijah as his successor.

Bob Deffenbaugh in his series of *Profiting from the Prophets* states that "Elisha was energized by the spirit that had once empowered Elijah." (2004-08-24)

Elisha had a great encounter, which resulted in being a recipient of the double anointing his master had. The transition of power flows from Moses, who parted the red sea, to his successor, Joshua, who also parted Jordan River. As Moses did heal waters at Marah, Elisha also healed the water of spring at Jericho. Greater works than Moses and Elijah did Elisha. He was strategically located, never to miss the double anointing.

Response

Elisha's ministry was filled with signs and wonders as a result of his encounter with the Holy Spirit. He was fully immersed in the supernatural power of God's Spirit. The Holy Spirit makes the difference in all things.

Challenge

In what way are you serving God to be positioned in alignment with his purpose for your life? What are you willing to give up for the sake of being a disciple of Christ?

CHAPTER 5

The Great Catch

With no prior knowledge about fishing, I have learned a lot from the story of Simon Peter, a fisherman turned fisher of men. A man whose profile can never be erased from the heart of believer because of his walk with Christ, and the divine revelation he had about Christ as the Messiah and Son of God. This Simon Peter was an ordinary man who grew up like every other person with an unknown background. An ordinary fisherman with a low profile who was called after an encounter with Jesus while engaging in his daily business activities. Peter, unlike Jeremiah and John the Baptist, was unknown with no prior prophecy concerning his birth. Jesus's passion for discipleship and Peter's positive attitude produced a synergistic effect that resulted to satisfaction on both sides; Jesus had a big catch of a fisher of men, and Peter had a net-breaking overload of fish.

Peter's encounter with Christ is being displayed in the mirror world that extends through an elaborate pattern of his fishing lifestyle. In this plot twist, Peter was seeking to catch fish while Jesus was seeking a platform to preach the Gospel. Although their desires varied, they were both seeking an opportunity to fill a vacuum of need. There are two important things to note in this story. The "passion" and "positive attitude" which are required for a successful assignment. Someone once said, "Passion is all there's to fishing," and I say, "What is more to winning souls?" Passion.

In Jesus's case, his passion is for winning souls for the kingdom while Peter's passion is to fish and catch enough to sell and make profits. Keeping a positive attitude is a necessity in catching a lot of fishes says a writer because those who believe they will catch a lot of fishes will exceptionally do. Jesus's meeting with Peter was not a coincidence, rather it was divinely arranged. Comparing Jesus, the exceptionally excellent fisher of men to Peter, an experienced fisherman, one could easily conclude that the goal is to catch something precious and extraordinary.

Positive Attitude

A positive attitude attracts positivity. There are seasons in our lives where positive attitude becomes a challenge due to the difficulty we are facing. The power of positive attitude can never be understated. This was the attitude Peter had despite his inability to catch a fish after toiling all night. He had lost hope and decided to wash his net. Jesus entered his boat to use it as a preaching platform, and He beckoned on Peter to push the boat off shore, which he did. After Jesus's preaching, He said to Peter, "Put out into the deep water and lower your nets for a catch." Because Peter was an experienced fisherman, he lamented to Jesus that he had tried all night but caught nothing. However, at Jesus's word, he gave it a try, an obedience which produced a bountiful and net-breaking harvest. Jesus was able to fulfill His assignment in reaching out to the lost souls who were crowding around Him. How hospitable are you when Jesus knocks on the door of your heart? Is your heart a platform for God like Peter's boat?

After Peter's exposure to a net-breaking miracle, he realized he had experienced a supernatural act of God. Then he realized how sinful he was. Jesus responded with grace, and Peter became one of Jesus's disciples. There are series of events which shows Peter's imperfect nature, nevertheless, Jesus never gave up on him. Peter's realm of strength was challenged when Jesus was arrested to be crucified. Peter who had boasted that he would never deny Jesus ended up denying him three times publicly. At this time, Peter lacked the ministry of the Holy Spirit which helps us stay committed to our promises. We know our human flesh is always weak, but the Spirit is willing to help our infirmities.

> Stay alert; be in prayer so you don't wander into temptation without even knowing you're in danger. There is a part of you that is eager, ready for anything in God. But there's another part that's as lazy as an old dog sleeping by the fire. (Matthew 26:4)

How often have you fallen into the pit of sin? When we have an encounter with the Holy Spirit, we find ourselves being emptied, and we come to realize there is a vacuum to be filled. All these events happened before the day of Pentecost. Jesus admonishes His disciples to wait and tarry for the Holy Spirit because without him, they cannot have results. At Pentecost, there was a great change that traveled around the city where the disciples were. The spirit divided himself as a tongue of fire and filled the upper room. The Peter who denied ever walking with Christ was transformed after an encounter with the Holy Spirit at Pentecost. He began to preach the Gospel of Christ unashamedly because of his renewed mind and transformed heart.

He became the rock upon which Christ's church was built. Most times, we need that second touch in our lives after we are saved. Encounter with Christ does not have to be once, it is continuous. Having a deeper knowledge of who Christ is through steady encounter with the *Jesus-revealed* is endless in our spiritual growth as Christians. Peter's insight moved from ordinary to extraordinary while working in the supernatural because something great had happened to him. He began to walk in God's revelation and in a higher realm beyond the capacity of his own strength.

Response

Peter became a fisher of men, tending and feeding the lambs of God as Christ instructed him. The ever-passive Peter began to preach about Christ with passion and conviction through the power of God's spirit in him.

Challenge

Can we see ourselves in Peter's reflection? Can you step out boldly for Christ? Are you speaking the undiluted truth in the Word of God? Are you feeding and tending the sheep of the master?

Chapter 6

At Master's Feet

According to one of the beatitudes which is the Sermon on the Mount, Jesus talked about those who hunger and thirst after righteousness for they shall be satisfied. Such was the reward of Mary of Bethany who humbled herself at the feet of the Master to grasp the knowledge of Christ. Her priority goes beyond the physical fulfillment. Mary's attitude depicts hunger and thirst for spiritual knowledge of who the Lord is. She had a personal encounter with Christ in the comfort of her home where she sat to be fed the bread of life needed in life's long journey. Her longing for fellowship and communion brought a life transformational change to her life. No wonder Charles Wesley wrote in "O Love Divine, How Sweet Thou Art" about Mary's choice with the master.

> Oh, that I could forever sit
> Like Mary, at the Master's feet
> Be this my happy choice;
> My only care, delight, and bliss,
> My joy, my rest on earth be this,
> To hear the Bridegroom's voice.

Widening one's perspective or frame of mind pertaining to relationship with Christ is encouraged because it results to healthy spiritual living. Studying the life of one of the biblical aces, Mary of Bethany, one would discover a woman of humility, broaden outlook, and quest for spiritual knowledge in order to be spiritually fit. The Bible also recorded the profiles of people who met with Jesus, but Mary of Bethany's profile was one that can never be forgotten as Jesus emphasized that her memories will be told as far as the Gospel is preached. Valuable lessons can be learned from studying her life.

The Will

This is a position of willingness to fellowship with the Master. Our quest to know more about the Lord always brings us to a place of deep fellowship with Him. Communing with the Master is beyond physical attention to words from the altar or reading the Word of God, but the will to know and learn more is a necessity in our fellowship. As Christians, we must be willing to unlearn many things in order to learn new things about the Savior. This encounter which Mary had was not as a result of someone feeding her with the milk of the word, but it was a personal encounter with the Savior Himself, which was birthed through her will to know more. The more we seek the Master, the more we find Him. Martha, unlike her sister, Mary, was busy with domestic services and hospitality, worried over many things to satisfy the physical demand of the visitors in their home. Her priority set her off the essential which Mary had chosen.

Humility

A good act of acknowledging ignorance and lowering oneself to be elated by the Master. Mary's attitude depicts that she did not overlook the presence of Christ in their home but realized it's an opportunity to encounter the Master Himself. Both worshipping God and serving God demands a humble attitude. To have an encounter with God, we need to come to a position of emptiness to be filled with Christ. It was in this low estate that Mary placed herself, and the resulting reward was enormous.

Focus

If there is one character who remained focused in her dealing with the Master, it's Mary of Bethany. Despite her sister scolding her for not joining her in her hospitality activities, she was only concerned with learning from the Lord. Likewise, her worship service in anointing Jesus's feet with aromatic oils. Judas rebuked her, but she continued with her actions. She allowed Jesus to defend her in these two instances while she focused on building a relationship with the Master. These act of service and worship memorized through ages, and we can boldly say Mary of Bethany is an example of house on the rock according to the parable of Jesus which weathered the storm of distraction and accusation for serving the Lord.

Response

In Mary's situation, after meeting the Lord and knowing the capacity of grace embedded in Christ, even in her grief, she trusted in her Master's arm as a place of solace. Despite the loss of her brother Lazarus, Mary left the assembly of mourners sympathizing with her to meet the Master when Jesus beckons on her. When in tribulation, we forget the words of the Master and focus on our present situations leaving us sinking in the pit of sorrow and worries. The essence of experiencing the Lord and His fullness is not for a limited time but for every situation we find ourselves at, any time all through our life's journey.

Challenge

Desire to sit at the feet of Jesus to seek him more. It promises great lifelong reward which can never be ignored.

> But seek first the kingdom of God and His righteousness, and all these things shall be added to you. (Matthew 6:33)

Chapter 7

Inside Out

How do you perceive extortionists and corrupt government officials who embezzle money meant for the development of the nation? They are named thieves, parasite, vampires, termites, caterpillars, and the list continues. They are being judged and abused at the slightest opportunity. Such was the case of the tax collectors who were hated for extorting money from their countrymen and also working for the foreign oppressors—the Romans. These tax officials were seen as traitors to their own people, hence they are not always popular. Zacchaeus was not just a tax collector but a chief tax collector who was wealthy through extortion of money from his countrymen. They cheated taxpayers and become wealthy through their dishonest jobs, so they get despised. These tax collectors do not receive a salary but would have a huge allowance after remitting a specific amount to the government while the remaining money goes to their pocket. They reap where they have not sown. This was a great deal of corruption.

As Jesus transited through Jericho, Zacchaeus was eager to see what Jesus's attention would be, but he ended up being the subject of attention. Zacchaeus was like a devoted fan of a star who knew the popular star couldn't have recognized him, but he desired to focus on the star. There was a twitch in Zacchaeus's heart, which prompted him to climb the sycamore fig tree in order to have the eagle view of Jesus. He was a short man who couldn't see Jesus while standing on his tiptoes or pushing his way through to the front of the crowd, like the blind man who called on "Jesus, son of David, have mercy on me." No one would have suggested to put him on their shoulders with his reputation. He sought after the best option he had, the sycamore tree. He was seeking to know who Jesus is while Jesus was prepared to reveal His purpose—to seek and save the lost. The willingness to know Jesus, which Zacchaeus felt in his heart, was the grace of God drawing him to Jesus, the Son of God.

As a hated outcast, Zacchaeus was not bothered about how people perceived him, but he focused more on the Savior.

The Meeting

When Jesus came to the sycamore tree, he beckoned on Zacchaeus to come down from the tree. Have you ever wonder how Jesus got to know his name? They had never met before, but Jesus knew everything there was to know about Zacchaeus.

> For you formed my inward parts; you covered me
> in my mother's womb. (Psalm 139:13)

Instantly, Zacchaeus got down from the tree, answering the call of his Shepherd and Savior. Zacchaeus was probably feeling all the emotions possible because Jesus found him. His human heart seeking God synced with God seeking to save his heart. This is grace at work. Jesus did not preach to Zacchaeus, but there was a transformation in his heart which led to a renewed lifestyle and restitution. An encounter is a heart-changing and mind-transforming experience which yields visible results. In reality, those who seek to know more about Jesus are sought, seen, and saved by their Savior.

How busy are you in seeking God when he beckons on you? Most of our daily activities have filled the spot of knowing more about God. Have you made it your quest to have an in-depth knowledge of who God is? God awaits our willingness to search for the treasure in Him, which can be found in knowing Him through fellowshipping with Him. But how can you commune with the one you do not have a relationship with? We are likened to Zacchaeus until we accept his invitation. Jesus inviting himself as a guest to a sinner's house or heart shows his acceptance which leads to forgiveness of sins and regeneration.

Restitution

There is always a positive outcome when we have an encounter with the son of God. We are never the same because of the transforming power of God at work in our lives. We become a new being as a result of old wineskins burst and replaced with new wineskin for our preservation. After spending time with Jesus, Zacchaeus became a completely changed man through his genuine repentance and Jesus's acceptance. It was an inward transformation and not a forced entry into Zacchaeus heart and home; God will never force Himself on anyone. A fisted hand or a filled hand has no space to take God's fullness. We, therefore, must let go of something in our hands and life to grasp the hand and fullness of Christ. There is a need to empty ourselves to be filled with God.

Unlike the rich ruler who sought eternal life for himself but not willing to let go of his wealth according to Jesus's word, Zacchaeus expressed his willingness to give half of his properties to the poor and refund in fourfold to everyone he had cheated. A man who was known to be a parasite identified his wrongness and willingly stated his intention to amend his ways. Identifying our wrong lifestyle and changing to a new life in Jesus is an expression of our new faith and walk with God. Those who murmured because Jesus invited Himself to be a guest in a sinner's house would begin to perceive the outcome of Zacchaeus's encounter with Jesus as a changed man. While the Jews ritually make themselves impure by communing with a sinner, Jesus purifies the sinner with His blood.

Response

Caterpillars are pests, which have a cutting and chewing mouth part that can be destructive if not prevented or treated early. They cause an exceptional damage to plants. They are creepy and greedy, always wanting to munch. When the caterpillar stops eating and hangs itself upside down from a leaf, it wholly transforms its body, hence emerging as a butterfly. What an amazing transformation! What has changed? Its lifestyle. Butterflies are beautiful creatures, mostly seen flying on a sunny summer day, and also have their fair share in pollinating flowers. We are likened to caterpillars before our encounter with Christ. It is Jesus who beautifies our lives, shines through us, and makes us emerge as a radically transformed new creature. We are changed from the inside out through the finished work of Christ in us.

Challenge

What lifestyle are you clinging to and not willing to let go? Letting go of so many things in our lives brings about a new man allowing God to work in us. Be transformed from the inside out!

> Neither do men put new wine into old bottles: else the bottles break, and the wine runneth out, and the bottles perish: but they put new wine into new bottles, and both are preserved. (Matthew 9:17)

Chapter 8

Bad Credit History

A bad credit history indicates a high-risk borrower who is most likely to fall behind if given a credit. They are charged a higher interest rate if approved. From human's perspective, this is the case of sinners who have been caught in the pit of their transgressions. Some utter the words while others wish in their hearts: he does not deserve mercy, jail him, and if possible, nail him. A once sinner, sanctified and redeemed by the blood of Jesus, calls another man a sinner, what an attitude! In this topic, the thief on the left side of Jesus at Calvary can be likened to a man with a bad credit history who deserved to be punished for his sins, but God's mercies caught up with him before he died. What an amazing grace and great encounter! This thief had no history recorded in the Bible, neither was his name ever written, but after meeting Christ, he had the hope of reigning with Christ in His kingdom.

Weakness Acknowledged

This thief knew who he was and acknowledged his weakness and bad ways. He believed he was justly rewarded for his bad deeds, unlike the other criminal, who condemned and blasphemed Jesus. Admitting our weaknesses is a great way to start working out our salvation. He acceded to his old ways but believed in the righteousness of Christ, even though they were all condemned to death.

> For with the heart man believeth unto righteousness; and with the mouth, confession is made unto salvation. (Romans 10:10)

The problem most people have is accepting their weaknesses. If we do not acknowledge our weaknesses, we can never let go and let God deal with them. Our free will is connected to accepting our feebleness, and until we allow God to deal with this fragility of ours, we cannot embrace His strength.

Priceless Opportunity

Surprisingly how we misuse valuable opportunities in our lives through procrastination. Delayed obedience or postponing activities range from short- to long-term negative result. This act can lead to lifelong regret with eternal consequence. As humans, one would believe this thief has reached the end of his life, and there is no redemption for his soul, but he utilized this valuable moment which turned out to be his transformational occasion with the hope of eternity. With no prior knowledge of Christ and no good work, he only had one thing—hope. He placed his eternal destiny and life into the hands of Jesus. He died in peace with Christ's promise that wiped out his pains and sorrows. Although he died a shameful death, he would be received in glory triumphantly.

There is a slight correlation between this story of the Bible and my grandfather in his last earthly days which I found to be a great testimony. This has been a great lesson of God's awesome work of salvation in redeeming souls.

My maternal grandfather was an occasional churchgoer. He listened to sermons in church but questioned the integrity of the Word mostly during sermons in church. Although he gave his children biblical names, taught them to attend church, but his belief in the Word of God was rootless. I can say he went to church religiously and as a ceremonious Christian. He believed in morals which is a great deal. However, there is a limit to a level you can grow to without Christ in your life. Jesus is the cream and the sweetest flavor to a sour and tasteless life. Prior to his death, God revealed to my mom that her dad would be saved through her household, and she started praying about it. My mom was abroad when her dad felt sick. We were all praying to God for his salvation before his death, with the hope that once my mom gets back home, she would be able to meet and lead him to Christ. Prior to his sickness, my dad with a pastor traveled to lead him to Christ, but as usual, he started questioning the integrity of the pastor and the Word of God.

Fast forward to his last sickness, without the presence of my mom, my dad together with the same pastor traveled down to my grandfather's house in our hometown to share the good news of Jesus with him, but this time, he accepted Jesus and was pleading for mercy. This was the greatest news I heard from home. My mom was overly joyous hearing that her father finally accepted Jesus. This happened about four to five days prior to his transition to glory. What a glorious exit! Our joy knew no bound as we rejoiced on earth that heaven received a new man. He lived 114 years without Christ, but just five days before he died, he received the gift of salvation. It was indeed a priceless moment. He did not miss the opportunity he had to encounter Christ, my dad didn't overlook the occasion of sharing Christ with him, and my mom did not delay her father's salvation awaiting her arrival. My grandfather died at about the same time my mom landed in my home country. She did not meet her father alive, but she was happy her father is resting in God's arm.

> For he saith, I have heard thee in a time accepted,
> and in the day of salvation have I succored thee:
> behold, now is the accepted time; behold, now is
> the day of salvation. (2 Corinthians 6:2)

It is therefore, a necessity to recognize, appreciate, and make the best use of every moment in our lives. There is no set time or place to have an encounter with the Lord. It may be convenient and comfortable or otherwise. Seize every moment as a priceless opportunity for delay may be too dangerous.

Response

The result of this encounter was heavenly. Transitioned to heaven gloriously with grace. The amazing grace and mercy of God at work, which blotted the transgression of an old wretched sinner with a bad history, and transformed him to a new Christ-centered, grace-filled, and heaven-bound man. Encounter always comes with newness and spiritual metamorphosis done by supernatural experience.

Challenge

Aspire to be heaven-bound by acknowledging your weakness and exchanging them for the strength of the Lord.

Seize every occasion to draw near to God; the only instrument needed is a heart that longs for more of God.

> Seek ye the Lord while he may be found, call ye upon him while he is near. (Isaiah 55:6)

Chapter 9

An Altered Vessel

How many times have you embraced what you once condemned? Such was the case of Saul of Tarsus turned Apostle Paul. Paul, a pharisaic Jew turned Christian, on his way to fulfill an assignment against Christians who embraced the way, Jesus. Saul was known as a harmful and dangerous man who got authorization letter from the high priest to arrest Christians. His mission was to bring and bind all the Christians to Jerusalem for trial before the Sanhedrin. On Paul's way to Damascus to persecute Christians as he always does, he experienced a life-transforming event. He was subdued by a supernatural power, and he fell to the ground. Upon hearing a voice, he knew the voice was of a supernatural being whose authority and power exceeds that of the high priest who authorized him to wipe out the Christians. Saul became blind, and Jesus commanded him to go to Damascus while he awaits what he will do.

He was led to the city by his fellow sojourners where he waited for three days without food or water. Those three days would have been a time of reflection, confusion, and repentance for Saul, a persecutor restricted and held-bound by God. What kind of thoughts would have been running through Paul's mind all through the three days? Paul was stripped from his power, authority, and ability, he was subdued under the power of God. These three days were a period of breaking, reforming, and transformation. Like a clay in a potter's hand, Paul's heart was remade by God, even though it was previously formed into a definite shape which humanly thinking, it's impossible to alter. God mold Paul's heart to fit His desire and pleasure.

Although Paul thought he was working for God to bring to justice anyone who claimed Jesus as the Messiah, not knowing he was a practitioner of religious activities which made him lose focus on Jesus the true Messiah. This was the lifestyle of the Pharisees and Sadducees who believed in the written word of God in the scrolls and religious rituals in the temple but did not embrace the Messiah sent to them by God.

> As he journeyed he came near Damascus, and suddenly a light shone around him from heaven. Then he fell to the ground, and heard a voice saying to him, "Saul, Saul, why are you persecuting Me?"
>
> And he said, "Who are You, Lord?"
>
> Then the Lord said, "I am Jesus, whom you are persecuting. It is hard for you to kick against the goads."
>
> So he, trembling and astonished, said, "Lord, what do you want me to do?" (Acts 9:3–6)

Jesus's response to Paul persecuting Him denotes that Jesus identifies with us while we are being tried, tested, and persecuted. He is always with us all through the episodes of our lives. Judging by the actions of Paul toward Christians, it is very easy to condemn him, but Jesus's word concerning Paul as a chosen vessel was an affirmation. Paul became an apostle by revelation from God, not by appointment of men. It's a great lesson that God can use or call anyone he chooses, even a hard-hearted man.

> I will give you a new heart and put a new spirit within you; I will take the heart of stone out of your flesh and give you a heart of flesh. (Ezekiel 36:26)

Paul's encounter with the Lord qualified him to be an apostle, and he got to know Jesus as the promised Messiah. God, who knew Paul before he was conceived, had chosen Paul before he decided to pursue God after his encounter. Most times, when we decide to pursue our desires and goals, we end up fulfilling the mission of Christ. Paul ended up doing the exact opposite of what he intended to do. Paul, once a persecutor of the church of Christ, became Paul, a missionary for God. What an amazing transformation! Encounter does not have to be spectacular or in a movie trailer format, it may be quiet but always transformational. It is the same Christ who plays the role of a Savior in our lives and in Paul's life. However, our transformational experience may vary.

God had us in mind when he saved Paul. Need I say more? Paul's life was a package of amazing grace whose testimonies God want us to read about in the Christendom. Paul's admonition to the churches in the New Testament is a testimony that has traveled far beyond where Paul's feet trod. In our world today, there are lots of men whose heart are hardened and full of immoral acts. As a saved generation, we need to arise for the salvation of others inasmuch as God has helped us to walk in the fullness of His grace. As humans, we may condemn them, but has God condemned them? No. How, then, are we expected to rise for their salvation? Through prayers, intercession, admonition, and love. We should not be reluctant witnesses, rather we should be willing witnesses of Christ. Learning from the example of Ananias, one of the disciples in Damascus who knew how dangerous Paul was. In his vision, God told him to go in search of Paul to anoint him. Ananias knew Paul was harmful, and the thought of being executed came to him. However, he hearkened to the voice of God to minister to Paul, and the result today is unquantifiable.

> And in a vision he has seen a man named Ananias coming in and putting his hand on him, so that he might receive his sight.
>
> Then Ananias answered, "Lord, I have heard from many about this man, how much harm he has done to Your saints in Jerusalem. And here

he has authority from the chief priests to bind all
who call on Your name." (Acts 9:12–14)

In what way has religious activities blindfolded you from focusing on Jesus?

You may be Ananias who worked behind the scene while Paul worked publicly with multitudes, but they both fulfilled the assignment given to them by God.

Response

Saul of Tarsus was transformed from an attacker or wolf to Apostle Paul, a shepherd and protector of the Jesus's fold.

Challenge

Who are the Saul of Tarsus of this present age? Who are the Ananias of today? Are you a willing witness or reluctant witness?

Every Saul of Tarsus needs an Ananias from God to set them on the motion of their ministry.

Conclusion

An encounter is not an unrealistic imagination but a real experience of the supernatural. It is not by accident or chance or mistake, but it is divinely orchestrated by God Himself through His supernatural power. You should not feel bad if you are yet to have one; rather, keep trusting God for a supernatural walk with Him because it's an experience you should desire to have. It is not limited to spiritual leaders or a certain denomination; rather, it's for everyone whom God wants to call to a new life in Him. Our past mistakes, background, race, attitude, and beliefs are never barriers to encounter with God because His desires for us is to have a new life to walk perfectly in Him.

You may not see lightning or flashes like Paul, and you may not hear a voice like Samuel but may come in a soft nature. Don't think it's an imagination or your thoughts because it's a seed, which is planted, that needs to be nurtured to grow supernaturally. In the stories we have learned from, the outcomes of encounter build up faith in the lives of those involved. After an encounter with God, you will never remain the same because it is life-changing and transformational. You begin to move from an ankle level to full immersion in the supernatural. This also becomes evidenced in your walk with God. You can never recover from the impartation that comes with an encounter with God.

An encounter is a necessity. Need I say more? It's not a once in a lifetime, the more we seek God, the more we find him. He is closer than you think.

> And you will seek Me and find Me, when you search for Me with all your heart. (Jeremiah 29:13)

Paul's story made us understand that it's not only those who love Christ that have encounters because God can touch anyone with His sovereign power to be used to suit His pleasure like He did to Paul. Is there anyone you have given up on because you feel they are notorious? God's arm is not too short to pull him closer; there is no heart that God cannot transform or conform to his pleasurable will.

How then do I seek to encounter God?

Firstly, you need to surrender your heart and will to God. Confess Him as your Lord and Savior. Enthrone Him as the King of your heart.

Fervently communicate with God through prayers.

Study to know God more, and He will surely reveal Himself to you.

Desire to have a transforming experience through His supernatural power.

Dedicate your life to following and honoring God in all things.

About the Author

Abigael Akintola is the founder of Master's Feet Network and Convener of Light Up Conference. She is called to raise torchbearers of Christ in the world. Her passion is to see people reflecting the light and love of Christ beyond their circle of influence but to the world at large. Abigael, a Bible-believing Christian, believes in the Holy Spirit for full inspiration and guidance in all her activities. With a great passion for the kingdom of God, she operates a platform on social media as a means of reaching out to lost souls by sharing the heart and love of the Father to His children. She is a graduate of physiology and pharmacology from the University of Saskatchewan, Canada. She is married to an amazing man, Ezekiel Akintola, and blessed with a lovely daughter.

Email: abigael.akintola23@gmail.com
Facebook: https://www.facebook.com/abigael.oludeyi
Instagram: @abigael.akintola

To contact me in regard to my book, please email me at Info@mastersfeetnerwork.org or visit my website www.mastersfeetnetwork.org for more information.

CPSIA information can be obtained
at www.ICGtesting.com
Printed in the USA
LVHW112258070220
646297LV00001B/47